This journal belongs to

....

life is too short

live it

Date_____   Area _____

Country _____

Occasion_____
_____

Trip Description And Items Weather/ Miles/ Vehicle/ etc	Today's Agenda

What Would You Change Today?	What Is Tomorrow's Adventure?

Date_____ Area _____

Country _____

Occasion _____
_____

Trip Description And Items Weather/ Miles/ Vehicle/ etc	Today's Agenda

What Would You Change Today?

What Is Tomorrow's Adventure?

Date_____ Area _____

Country _____

Occasion_____
_____

Trip Description And Items Weather/ Miles/ Vehicle/ etc	Today's Agenda

What Would You Change Today?	What Is Tomorrow's Adventure?

Date_____ Area _____

Country _____

Occasion_____
_____

Trip Description And Items Weather/ Miles/ Vehicle/ etc	Today's Agenda

What Is Tomorrow's Adventure?

What Would You Change Today?

Date_____   Area _____

Country _____

Occasion_____
_____

Trip Description And Items Weather/ Miles/ Vehicle/ etc	Today's Agenda

What Would You Change Today?

What Is Tomorrow's Adventure?

Date_____   Area _____

Country _____

Occasion _____
_____

Trip Description And Items Weather/ Miles/ Vehicle/ etc	Today's Agenda

What Would You Change Today?	What Is Tomorrow's Adventure?

Date_____ Area _____

Country _____

Occasion_____
_____

Trip Description And Items Weather/ Miles/ Vehicle/ etc	Today's Agenda

What Would You Change Today?

What Is Tomorrow's Adventure?

Date _____ Area _____

Country _____

Occasion _____

_____

Trip Description And Items Weather/ Miles/ Vehicle/ etc	Today's Agenda

What Would You Change Today?	What Is Tomorrow's Adventure?

Date_____ Area _____

Country _____

Occasion _____
_____

Trip Description And Items Weather/ Miles/ Vehicle/ etc	Today's Agenda

What Would You Change Today?	What Is Tomorrow's Adventure?

Date _____ Area _____

Country _____

Occasion _____
_____

Trip Description And Items Weather/ Miles/ Vehicle/ etc	Today's Agenda

What Would You Change Today?	What Is Tomorrow's Adventure?

Date_____   Area _____

Country _____

Occasion_____
_____

Trip Description And Items Weather/ Miles/ Vehicle/ etc	Today's Agenda

What Would You Change Today?	What Is Tomorrow's Adventure?

Date _____   Area _____

Country _____

Occasion _____
_____

Trip Description And Items Weather/ Miles/ Vehicle/ etc	Today's Agenda

What Would You Change Today?

What Is Tomorrow's Adventure?

Date_____ Area _____

Country _____

Occasion_____
_____

Trip Description And Items Weather/ Miles/ Vehicle/ etc	Today's Agenda

What Would You Change Today?	What Is Tomorrow's Adventure?

Date _____ Area _____

Country _____

Occasion _____
_____

Trip Description And Items Weather/ Miles/ Vehicle/ etc	Today's Agenda

What Would You Change Today?	What Is Tomorrow's Adventure?

Date_____   Area _____

Country _____

Occasion_____
_____

Trip Description And Items Weather/ Miles/ Vehicle/ etc	Today's Agenda

What Would You Change Today?	What Is Tomorrow's Adventure?

Date _____   Area _____

Country _____

Occasion _____
_____

Trip Description And Items Weather/ Miles/ Vehicle/ etc	Today's Agenda

What Would You Change Today?	What Is Tomorrow's Adventure?

Date_____ Area _____

Country _____

Occasion_____

_____

Trip Description And Items Weather/ Miles/ Vehicle/ etc	Today's Agenda

What Would You Change Today?

What Is Tomorrow's Adventure?

Date_____ Area _____

Country _____

Occasion _____
_____

Trip Description And Items Weather/ Miles/ Vehicle/ etc	Today's Agenda

	What Is Tomorrow's Adventure?
What Would You Change Today?	

Date _____ Area _____

Country _____

Occasion _____
_____

Trip Description And Items Weather/ Miles/ Vehicle/ etc	Today's Agenda

What Would You Change Today?

What Is Tomorrow's Adventure?

Date _____ Area _____

Country _____

Occasion _____
_____

Trip Description And Items Weather/ Miles/ Vehicle/ etc	Today's Agenda

What Would You Change Today?	What Is Tomorrow's Adventure?

Date_____   Area _____

Country _____

Occasion_____
_____

Trip Description And Items Weather/ Miles/ Vehicle/ etc	Today's Agenda

What Would You Change Today?	What Is Tomorrow's Adventure?

Date_____ Area _____

Country _____

Occasion _____
_____

Trip Description And Items Weather/ Miles/ Vehicle/ etc	Today's Agenda

What Would You Change Today?

What Is Tomorrow's Adventure?

Date_____   Area _____

Country _____

Occasion_____
_____

Trip Description And Items Weather/ Miles/ Vehicle/ etc	Today's Agenda

What Would You Change Today?	What Is Tomorrow's Adventure?

Date_____   Area _____

Country _____

Occasion _____
_____

Trip Description And Items Weather/ Miles/ Vehicle/ etc	Today's Agenda

What Would You Change Today?	What Is Tomorrow's Adventure?

Date_____ Area _____

Country _____

Occasion_____
_____

Trip Description And Items Weather/ Miles/ Vehicle/ etc	Today's Agenda

What Is Tomorrow's Adventure?

What Would You Change Today?

Date_____ Area _____

Country _____

Occasion_____
_____

Trip Description And Items Weather/ Miles/ Vehicle/ etc	Today's Agenda

What Would You Change Today?

What Is Tomorrow's Adventure?

Date_____ Area _____

Country _____

Occasion _____
_____

Trip Description And Items Weather/ Miles/ Vehicle/ etc	Today's Agenda

What Would You Change Today?

What Is Tomorrow's Adventure?

Date _____   Area _____

Country _____

Occasion _____
_____

Trip Description And Items Weather/ Miles/ Vehicle/ etc	Today's Agenda

What Is Tomorrow's Adventure?

What Would You Change Today?

Date_____ Area _____

Country _____

Occasion_____
_____

Trip Description And Items Weather/ Miles/ Vehicle/ etc	Today's Agenda

What Would You Change Today?	What Is Tomorrow's Adventure?

Date_____ Area _____

Country _____

Occasion _____

_____

Trip Description And Items Weather/ Miles/ Vehicle/ etc	Today's Agenda

What Is Tomorrow's Adventure?

What Would You Change Today?

Date_____ Area _____

Country _____

Occasion_____

_____

Trip Description And Items Weather/ Miles/ Vehicle/ etc	Today's Agenda

	What Is Tomorrow's Adventure?
What Would You Change Today?	

Date _____ Area _____

Country _____

Occasion _____

_____

Trip Description And Items Weather/ Miles/ Vehicle/ etc	Today's Agenda

What Would You Change Today?	What Is Tomorrow's Adventure?

Date_____ Area _____

Country _____

Occasion_____
_____

Trip Description And Items Weather/ Miles/ Vehicle/ etc	Today's Agenda

What Would You Change Today?

What Is Tomorrow's Adventure?

Date_____ Area _____

Country _____

Occasion _____
_____

Trip Description And Items Weather/ Miles/ Vehicle/ etc	Today's Agenda

What Would You Change Today?	What Is Tomorrow's Adventure?

Date_____ Area _____

Country _____

Occasion_____

_____

Trip Description And Items Weather/ Miles/ Vehicle/ etc	Today's Agenda

What Would You Change Today?	What Is Tomorrow's Adventure?

Date_____ Area _____

Country _____

Occasion _____
_____

Trip Description And Items Weather/ Miles/ Vehicle/ etc	Today's Agenda

What Is Tomorrow's Adventure?

What Would You Change Today?

Date_____   Area _____

Country _____

Occasion_____

_____

Trip Description And Items Weather/ Miles/ Vehicle/ etc	Today's Agenda

What Would You Change Today?

What Is Tomorrow's Adventure?

Date_____ Area _____

Country _____

Occasion _____

Trip Description And Items Weather/ Miles/ Vehicle/ etc	Today's Agenda

What Would You Change Today?	What Is Tomorrow's Adventure?

Date_____   Area _____

Country _____

Occasion_____

_____

Trip Description And Items Weather/ Miles/ Vehicle/ etc	Today's Agenda

What Would You Change Today?	What Is Tomorrow's Adventure?

Date_____   Area _____

Country _____

Occasion _____
_____

Trip Description And Items Weather/ Miles/ Vehicle/ etc	Today's Agenda

What Would You Change Today?	What Is Tomorrow's Adventure?

Date_____ Area _____

Country _____

Occasion _____
_____

Trip Description And Items Weather/ Miles/ Vehicle/ etc	Today's Agenda

What Would You Change Today?

What Is Tomorrow's Adventure?

Date_____   Area _____

Country _____

Occasion_____
_____

Trip Description And Items Weather/ Miles/ Vehicle/ etc	Today's Agenda

What Would You Change Today?	What Is Tomorrow's Adventure?

Date_____ Area _____

Country _____

Occasion_____
_____

Trip Description And Items Weather/ Miles/ Vehicle/ etc	Today's Agenda

What Would You Change Today?	What Is Tomorrow's Adventure?

Date _____   Area _____

Country _____

Occasion _____
_____

Trip Description And Items Weather/ Miles/ Vehicle/ etc	Today's Agenda

What Would You Change Today?	What Is Tomorrow's Adventure?

Date_____ Area _____

Country _____

Occasion_____
_____

Trip Description And Items Weather/ Miles/ Vehicle/ etc	Today's Agenda

What Would You Change Today?

What Is Tomorrow's Adventure?

Date_____   Area _____

Country _____

Occasion _____

_____

Trip Description And Items Weather/ Miles/ Vehicle/ etc	Today's Agenda

What Would You Change Today?	What Is Tomorrow's Adventure?

Date_____ Area _____

Country _____

Occasion_____
_____

Trip Description And Items Weather/ Miles/ Vehicle/ etc	Today's Agenda

What Would You Change Today?	What Is Tomorrow's Adventure?

Date_____   Area _____

Country _____

Occasion_____
_____

Trip Description And Items Weather/ Miles/ Vehicle/ etc	Today's Agenda

What Would You Change Today?	What Is Tomorrow's Adventure?

Date _____ Area _____

Country _____

Occasion _____
_____

Trip Description And Items Weather/ Miles/ Vehicle/ etc	Today's Agenda

What Would You Change Today?	What Is Tomorrow's Adventure?

Date_____ Area _____

Country _____

Occasion_____

_____

Trip Description And Items Weather/ Miles/ Vehicle/ etc	Today's Agenda

What Would You Change Today?

What Is Tomorrow's Adventure?

Date_____ Area _____

Country _____

Occasion_____
_____

Trip Description And Items Weather/ Miles/ Vehicle/ etc	Today's Agenda

What Is Tomorrow's Adventure?

What Would You Change Today?

Date _____ Area _____

Country _____

Occasion _____
_____

Trip Description And Items Weather/ Miles/ Vehicle/ etc	Today's Agenda

	What Is Tomorrow's Adventure?

What Would You Change Today?	

Date_____ Area _____

Country _____

Occasion_____
_____

Trip Description And Items Weather/ Miles/ Vehicle/ etc	Today's Agenda

What Would You Change Today?

What Is Tomorrow's Adventure?

Date _____ Area _____

Country _____

Occasion _____
_____

Trip Description And Items Weather/ Miles/ Vehicle/ etc	Today's Agenda

What Would You Change Today?	What Is Tomorrow's Adventure?

Date_____ Area _____

Country _____

Occasion_____
_____

Trip Description And Items Weather/ Miles/ Vehicle/ etc	Today's Agenda

What Would You Change Today?

What Is Tomorrow's Adventure?

Date_____   Area _____

Country _____

Occasion _____

_____

Trip Description And Items Weather/ Miles/ Vehicle/ etc	Today's Agenda

What Would You Change Today?

What Is Tomorrow's Adventure?

Date_____ Area _____

Country _____

Occasion_____
_____

Trip Description And Items Weather/ Miles/ Vehicle/ etc	Today's Agenda

What Would You Change Today?	What Is Tomorrow's Adventure?

Date_____   Area _____

Country _____

Occasion_____
_____

Trip Description And Items Weather/ Miles/ Vehicle/ etc	Today's Agenda

What Would You Change Today?	What Is Tomorrow's Adventure?

Date_____ Area _____

Country _____

Occasion_____

_____

Trip Description And Items Weather/ Miles/ Vehicle/ etc	Today's Agenda

What Would You Change Today?

What Is Tomorrow's Adventure?

Date _____ Area _____

Country _____

Occasion _____
_____

Trip Description And Items Weather/ Miles/ Vehicle/ etc	Today's Agenda

What Would You Change Today?	What Is Tomorrow's Adventure?

Date_____ Area _____

Country _____

Occasion_____
_____

Trip Description And Items Weather/ Miles/ Vehicle/ etc	Today's Agenda

What Would You Change Today?	What Is Tomorrow's Adventure?

Date_____   Area _____

Country _____

Occasion_____

_____

Trip Description And Items Weather/ Miles/ Vehicle/ etc	Today's Agenda

What Would You Change Today?

What Is Tomorrow's Adventure?

Date_____   Area _____

Country _____

Occasion_____

_____

Trip Description And Items Weather/ Miles/ Vehicle/ etc	Today's Agenda

What Would You Change Today?

What Is Tomorrow's Adventure?

Date_____   Area _____

Country _____

Occasion_____
_____

Trip Description And Items Weather/ Miles/ Vehicle/ etc	Today's Agenda

What Would You Change Today?	What Is Tomorrow's Adventure?

Date_____   Area _____

Country _____

Occasion_____

_____

Trip Description And Items Weather/ Miles/ Vehicle/ etc	Today's Agenda

What Would You Change Today?

What Is Tomorrow's Adventure?

Date_____   Area _____

Country _____

Occasion_____
_____

Trip Description And Items Weather/ Miles/ Vehicle/ etc	Today's Agenda

What Would You Change Today?	What Is Tomorrow's Adventure?

Date_____   Area _____

Country _____

Occasion_____

_____

Trip Description And Items Weather/ Miles/ Vehicle/ etc	Today's Agenda

What Would You Change Today?

What Is Tomorrow's Adventure?

Date_____   Area _____

Country _____

Occasion _____

_____

Trip Description And Items Weather/ Miles/ Vehicle/ etc	Today's Agenda

What Would You Change Today?	What Is Tomorrow's Adventure?

Date_____ Area _____

Country _____

Occasion_____
_____

Trip Description And Items Weather/ Miles/ Vehicle/ etc	Today's Agenda

What Is Tomorrow's Adventure?

What Would You Change Today?

Date_____ Area _____

Country _____

Occasion _____

_____

Trip Description And Items Weather/ Miles/ Vehicle/ etc	Today's Agenda

What Would You Change Today?

What Is Tomorrow's Adventure?

Date _____ Area _____

Country _____

Occasion _____
_____

Trip Description And Items Weather/ Miles/ Vehicle/ etc	Today's Agenda

What Would You Change Today?	What Is Tomorrow's Adventure?

Date_____   Area _____

Country _____

Occasion_____

_____

Trip Description And Items Weather/ Miles/ Vehicle/ etc	Today's Agenda

What Would You Change Today?	What Is Tomorrow's Adventure?

Date_____ Area _____

Country _____

Occasion_____
_____

Trip Description And Items Weather/ Miles/ Vehicle/ etc	Today's Agenda

What Would You Change Today?

What Is Tomorrow's Adventure?

Date_____ Area _____

Country _____

Occasion _____
_____

Trip Description And Items Weather/ Miles/ Vehicle/ etc	Today's Agenda

What Is Tomorrow's Adventure?

What Would You Change Today?

Date_____   Area _____

Country _____

Occasion_____
_____

Trip Description And Items Weather/ Miles/ Vehicle/ etc	Today's Agenda

What Would You Change Today?

What Is Tomorrow's Adventure?

Date_____ Area _____

Country _____

Occasion_____
_____

Trip Description And Items Weather/ Miles/ Vehicle/ etc	Today's Agenda

What Would You Change Today?	What Is Tomorrow's Adventure?

Date_____ Area _____

Country _____

Occasion_____
_____

Trip Description And Items Weather/ Miles/ Vehicle/ etc	Today's Agenda

What Would You Change Today?	What Is Tomorrow's Adventure?

Date _____ Area _____

Country _____

Occasion _____
_____

Trip Description And Items Weather/ Miles/ Vehicle/ etc	Today's Agenda

What Would You Change Today?	What Is Tomorrow's Adventure?

Date_____   Area _____

Country _____

Occasion_____
_____

Trip Description And Items Weather/ Miles/ Vehicle/ etc	Today's Agenda

What Would You Change Today?	What Is Tomorrow's Adventure?

Date _____ Area _____

Country _____

Occasion _____
_____

Trip Description And Items Weather/ Miles/ Vehicle/ etc	Today's Agenda

What Would You Change Today?	What Is Tomorrow's Adventure?

Date _____ Area _____

Country _____

Occasion _____
_____

Trip Description And Items Weather/ Miles/ Vehicle/ etc	Today's Agenda

What Would You Change Today?	What Is Tomorrow's Adventure?

Date_____   Area _____

Country _____

Occasion_____
_____

Trip Description And Items Weather/ Miles/ Vehicle/ etc	Today's Agenda

What Would You Change Today?	What Is Tomorrow's Adventure?

Date_____ Area _____

Country _____

Occasion_____
_____

Trip Description And Items Weather/ Miles/ Vehicle/ etc	Today's Agenda

What Would You Change Today?	What Is Tomorrow's Adventure?

Date_____ Area _____

Country _____

Occasion_____
_____

Trip Description And Items Weather/ Miles/ Vehicle/ etc	Today's Agenda

What Would You Change Today?

What Is Tomorrow's Adventure?

Date _____ Area _____

Country _____

Occasion _____
_____

Trip Description And Items Weather/ Miles/ Vehicle/ etc	Today's Agenda

What Is Tomorrow's Adventure?

What Would You Change Today?

Date_____   Area _____

Country _____

Occasion _____
_____

Trip Description And Items Weather/ Miles/ Vehicle/ etc	Today's Agenda

What Is Tomorrow's Adventure?

What Would You Change Today?

Date_____ Area _____

Country _____

Occasion_____
_____

Trip Description And Items Weather/ Miles/ Vehicle/ etc	Today's Agenda

What Would You Change Today?

What Is Tomorrow's Adventure?

Date_____ Area _____

Country _____

Occasion _____
_____

Trip Description And Items Weather/ Miles/ Vehicle/ etc	Today's Agenda

What Would You Change Today?

What Is Tomorrow's Adventure?

Date_____ Area _____

Country _____

Occasion_____
_____

Trip Description And Items Weather/ Miles/ Vehicle/ etc	Today's Agenda

What Would You Change Today?	What Is Tomorrow's Adventure?

Date _____ Area _____

Country _____

Occasion _____
_____

Trip Description And Items Weather/ Miles/ Vehicle/ etc	Today's Agenda

What Is Tomorrow's Adventure?

What Would You Change Today?

Date_____ Area _____

Country _____

Occasion_____
_____

Trip Description And Items Weather/ Miles/ Vehicle/ etc	Today's Agenda

What Is Tomorrow's Adventure?

What Would You Change Today?

Date _____ Area _____

Country _____

Occasion _____
_____

Trip Description And Items Weather/ Miles/ Vehicle/ etc	Today's Agenda

What Would You Change Today?	What Is Tomorrow's Adventure?

Date_____   Area _____

Country _____

Occasion_____
_____

Trip Description And Items Weather/ Miles/ Vehicle/ etc	Today's Agenda

What Would You Change Today?	What Is Tomorrow's Adventure?

Date_____   Area _____

Country _____

Occasion_____

Trip Description And Items Weather/ Miles/ Vehicle/ etc	Today's Agenda

What Would You Change Today?	What Is Tomorrow's Adventure?

Date_____ Area _____

Country _____

Occasion_____
_____

Trip Description And Items Weather/ Miles/ Vehicle/ etc	Today's Agenda

What Is Tomorrow's Adventure?

What Would You Change Today?

Date_____ Area _____

Country _____

Occasion_____
_____

Trip Description And Items Weather/ Miles/ Vehicle/ etc	Today's Agenda

What Would You Change Today?	What Is Tomorrow's Adventure?

Date_____ Area _____

Country _____

Occasion_____

_____

Trip Description And Items Weather/ Miles/ Vehicle/ etc	Today's Agenda

What Would You Change Today?

What Is Tomorrow's Adventure?

Date_____ Area _____

Country _____

Occasion_____
_____

Trip Description And Items Weather/ Miles/ Vehicle/ etc	Today's Agenda

What Would You Change Today?	What Is Tomorrow's Adventure?

Date_____ Area _____

Country _____

Occasion_____
_____

Trip Description And Items Weather/ Miles/ Vehicle/ etc	Today's Agenda

What Would You Change Today?

What Is Tomorrow's Adventure?

Date_____ Area _____

Country _____

Occasion_____
_____

Trip Description And Items Weather/ Miles/ Vehicle/ etc	Today's Agenda

What Would You Change Today?	What Is Tomorrow's Adventure?

Date_____ Area _____

Country _____

Occasion_____
_____

Trip Description And Items Weather/ Miles/ Vehicle/ etc	Today's Agenda

What Would You Change Today?

What Is Tomorrow's Adventure?

Date_____   Area _____

Country _____

Occasion _____
_____

Trip Description And Items Weather/ Miles/ Vehicle/ etc	Today's Agenda

What Would You Change Today?	What Is Tomorrow's Adventure?

Date_____   Area _____

Country _____

Occasion_____
_____

Trip Description And Items Weather/ Miles/ Vehicle/ etc	Today's Agenda

What Would You Change Today?	What Is Tomorrow's Adventure?

Date_____   Area _____

Country _____

Occasion _____
_____

Trip Description And Items Weather/ Miles/ Vehicle/ etc	Today's Agenda

What Would You Change Today?	What Is Tomorrow's Adventure?

Date_____ Area _____

Country _____

Occasion_____

_____

Trip Description And Items Weather/ Miles/ Vehicle/ etc	Today's Agenda

What Would You Change Today?

What Is Tomorrow's Adventure?

Date_____ Area _____

Country _____

Occasion _____
_____

Trip Description And Items Weather/ Miles/ Vehicle/ etc	Today's Agenda

What Would You Change Today?

What Is Tomorrow's Adventure?

Date_____ Area _____

Country _____

Occasion_____
_____

Trip Description And Items Weather/ Miles/ Vehicle/ etc	Today's Agenda

What Is Tomorrow's Adventure?

What Would You Change Today?

Date _____   Area _____

Country _____

Occasion _____
_____

Trip Description And Items Weather/ Miles/ Vehicle/ etc	Today's Agenda

What Would You Change Today?	What Is Tomorrow's Adventure?

Date_____ Area _____

Country _____

Occasion_____
_____

Trip Description And Items Weather/ Miles/ Vehicle/ etc	Today's Agenda

What Would You Change Today?

What Is Tomorrow's Adventure?

Date_____ Area _____

Country _____

Occasion _____
_____

Trip Description And Items Weather/ Miles/ Vehicle/ etc	Today's Agenda

What Would You Change Today?	What Is Tomorrow's Adventure?

Date_____ Area _____

Country _____

Occasion_____
_____

Trip Description And Items Weather/ Miles/ Vehicle/ etc	Today's Agenda

What Would You Change Today?	What Is Tomorrow's Adventure?

Date_____ Area _____

Country _____

Occasion_____
_____

Trip Description And Items Weather/ Miles/ Vehicle/ etc	Today's Agenda

What Would You Change Today?	What Is Tomorrow's Adventure?

Date_____   Area _____

Country _____

Occasion_____
_____

Trip Description And Items Weather/ Miles/ Vehicle/ etc	Today's Agenda

What Would You Change Today?	What Is Tomorrow's Adventure?

Date_____ Area _____

Country _____

Occasion_____
_____

Trip Description And Items Weather/ Miles/ Vehicle/ etc	Today's Agenda

What Would You Change Today?

What Is Tomorrow's Adventure?

Date _____ Area _____

Country _____

Occasion _____

_____

Trip Description And Items Weather/ Miles/ Vehicle/ etc	Today's Agenda

What Would You Change Today?

What Is Tomorrow's Adventure?

Date_____   Area _____

Country _____

Occasion_____
_____

Trip Description And Items Weather/ Miles/ Vehicle/ etc	Today's Agenda

What Would You Change Today?	What Is Tomorrow's Adventure?

Date_____ Area _____

Country _____

Occasion_____
_____

Trip Description And Items Weather/ Miles/ Vehicle/ etc	Today's Agenda

What Would You Change Today?	What Is Tomorrow's Adventure?

Date_____ Area _____

Country _____

Occasion _____
_____

Trip Description And Items Weather/ Miles/ Vehicle/ etc	Today's Agenda

What Would You Change Today?	What Is Tomorrow's Adventure?

Date_____   Area _____

Country _____

Occasion_____

_____

Trip Description And Items Weather/ Miles/ Vehicle/ etc	Today's Agenda

What Would You Change Today?	What Is Tomorrow's Adventure?

Made in the USA
Las Vegas, NV
16 April 2022

47561527R00068